BOA
EDITIONS
LIMITED

Song by Brigit Pegeen Kelly is the 1994 Lamont Poetry Selection of The Academy of American Poets.

From 1954 through 1974 the Lamont Poetry Selection supported the publication and distribution of a first collection of poems. Since 1975 this distinguished award has been given for an American poet's second book.

Judges for 1994:
Jorie Graham, Richard Kenney, David St. John

SONG

Poems by
Brigit Pegeen Kelly

BOA Editions Ltd. ⌣ Brockport, NY ⌣ 1995

LC #: 94–72746
ISBN: 1–880238–12–8 cloth
ISBN: 1–880238–13–6 paper

First Edition
95 96 97 98   7 6 5 4 3 2 1

The publication of books by BOA Editions, Ltd.,
is made possible with the assistance of grants from
the Literature Program of the New York State Council on the Arts
and the Literature Program of the National Endowment for the Arts,
as well as from the Lannan Foundation, the Lila Wallace–Reader's Digest
Literary Publishers Marketing Development Program,
the Rochester Area Foundation, the County of Monroe, NY, and contributions
by individual supporters.

Cover Design: Daphne Poulin
Typesetting: R. Foerster, York Beach, ME
Manufacturing: McNaughton & Gunn, Lithographers
BOA Logo: Mirko

BOA Editions, Ltd.
A. Poulin, Jr., President
92 Park Avenue
Brockport, NY 14420

for Huck, Maria, and Macklin

and for Michael

⁓

Contents

III

IV

SONG

I

Song

Listen: there was a goat's head hanging by ropes in a tree.
All night it hung there and sang. And those who heard it
Felt a hurt in their hearts and thought they were hearing
The song of a night bird. They sat up in their beds, and then
They lay back down again. In the night wind, the goat's head
Swayed back and forth, and from far off it shone faintly
The way the moonlight shone on the train track miles away
Beside which the goat's headless body lay. Some boys
Had hacked its head off. It was harder work than they had imagined.
The goat cried like a man and struggled hard. But they
Finished the job. They hung the bleeding head by the school
And then ran off into the darkness that seems to hide everything.
The head hung in the tree. The body lay by the tracks.
The head called to the body. The body to the head.
They missed each other. The missing grew large between them,
Until it pulled the heart right out of the body, until
The drawn heart flew toward the head, flew as a bird flies
Back to its cage and the familiar perch from which it trills.
Then the heart sang in the head, softly at first and then louder,
Sang long and low until the morning light came up over
The school and over the tree, and then the singing stopped....
The goat had belonged to a small girl. She named
The goat Broken Thorn Sweet Blackberry, named it after
The night's bush of stars, because the goat's silky hair
Was dark as well water, because it had eyes like wild fruit.
The girl lived near a high railroad track. At night
She heard the trains passing, the sweet sound of the train's horn
Pouring softly over her bed, and each morning she woke
To give the bleating goat his pail of warm milk. She sang
Him songs about girls with ropes and cooks in boats.
She brushed him with a stiff brush. She dreamed daily
That he grew bigger, and he did. She thought her dreaming
Made it so. But one night the girl didn't hear the train's horn,
And the next morning she woke to an empty yard. The goat
Was gone. Everything looked strange. It was as if a storm

Had passed through while she slept, wind and stones, rain
Stripping the branches of fruit. She knew that someone
Had stolen the goat and that he had come to harm. She called
To him. All morning and into the afternoon, she called
And called. She walked and walked. In her chest a bad feeling
Like the feeling of the stones gouging the soft undersides
Of her bare feet. Then somebody found the goat's body
By the high tracks, the flies already filling their soft bottles
At the goat's torn neck. Then somebody found the head
Hanging in a tree by the school. They hurried to take
These things away so that the girl would not see them.
They hurried to raise money to buy the girl another goat.
They hurried to find the boys who had done this, to hear
Them say it was a joke, a joke, it was nothing but a joke....
But listen: here is the point. The boys thought to have
Their fun and be done with it. It was harder work than they
Had imagined, this silly sacrifice, but they finished the job,
Whistling as they washed their large hands in the dark.
What they didn't know was that the goat's head was already
Singing behind them in the tree. What they didn't know
Was that the goat's head would go on singing, just for them,
Long after the ropes were down, and that they would learn to listen,
Pail after pail, stroke after patient stroke. They would
Wake in the night thinking they heard the wind in the trees
Or a night bird, but their hearts beating harder. There
Would be a whistle, a hum, a high murmur, and, at last, a song,
The low song a lost boy sings remembering his mother's call.
Not a cruel song, no, no, not cruel at all. This song
Is sweet. It is sweet. The heart dies of this sweetness.

⌣

Of Royal Issue

The sun only a small bird flitting, a wren
    in the stripped forsythia, of little
note. A boy stands and watches it for a moment
    but then he loses interest and cuts
across the dull winter grass to play a game
    with a stick and a rock and soft repeated
shouts, and the bird is nothing again
    but a brown thing, within a fabric of brown
branches, mind and heart, the cages of.
    Days and days from now, each a web
of small branches, in the weeks of high wet
    winds that bring out low patches
of wild onion along the swollen creek
    and call up countless red-bellied birds
to dibble the grass with their blunt beaks,
    the bush's royal bloodline will briefly show,
a tide of gold, a small inland sea, and the wren
    will speak for it, words of royal issue,
tongue after tongue, worthy of note.
    But now the bush is mute. Our common blood
slows but will not sleep, a kind of footpath
    the mind trudges over, back and forth,
back and forth, packing the cold dirt down.... O little bird,
    how small you are, small enough to fit in a palm,
no contender, a featherweight. Perhaps
    we can pay the boy to trick you out of the bush,
and trap you, and bring you in to this spot
    by the window where your little song may
amount to more than a tablespoon's worth of salt.
    The glass will quicken your call, multiply it,
multiply your nervous figure and your habit
    of play, until you are not one bird but a hundred,
not one tongue but a thousand, sweet prophesy
    of the wind lighting the white strips
of the bed sheets the boy will tear and tie

     to the black branches of all the garden's
trees, for no reason, because his hands
          will not stop, *bird in the mind, bird in the bush,*
the bird of the blood brightening
          as it calls and calls for its mate.

The Column of Mercury
Recording the Temperature of Night

No sleep in the night. No Sleep prowling like a caged animal.
And the smell of hyacinth heady in the air. Seductive.
Flirtatious. A mummery of scent. A museum of scent:

The wax figure house of things better forgotten. There
Are carved lions on the lawn but they offer small protection.
The lions hold up the stone table, the thick slate table

Like the tablets of the law engraved on the heart. *Each*
Man who eats sour grapes, his teeth shall be set on edge.
Or the tablets we take to sleep, whose carved words

Are about the erasure of other words. A kind of forgiveness.
The baby bleats. All night. No Sleep in his wolf suit
Shuttling back and forth, back and forth, a dark habitant,

Like the train crossing the landscape. The landscape is flat
But still the melancholy grows steeper. And the train
Slows in the night. There is no station here, but the train

Takes a long slowing. It makes a flutelike sound: a sound
Like held breath escaping, or the last drops falling
From a cloth wrung so tightly that it can be wrung no more.

Beside the hospital the giant flag blows out in soft decorum.
And then folds down like a bush or an abashed bird
As the train crosses before it. Blots it out. The train

Like a shovel in the garden. The train like a suited cadaver
In a coffin. All proper and on schedule. Though
There is no station here. Though the sound of the train slowing

Is like the sound of a flute played not by lips but by wind.
The hospital is a white dream, an unfathomable chalk cliff
With dark caves in it. A garden of sleeplessness. A garden

Full of sleep eaters and the audience they have captured:
The ones they hurt as they eat the heart's carved tablets.
And then eat the memory of them. A kind of forgiveness.

No sleep and the body shudders. The body's heat diminishes.
The unsocked feet grow cold. The child bleats. Is it hate
Does this? Oh, yes, probably. But how can we guess at it?

The depths of it? The train passes. The flag pours out
Again in slow motion.... White fleece of moonlight.
No, the moonlight is dirty lamb's wool. Something a child

Sucked on and then dropped behind her on the tracks.
Paired tracks. Twinned. Locked, like the carved lions
On the lawn, in the small posture of their destiny.

A Live Dog Being Better Than a Dead Lion

Rain. Rain from Baltimore. The ballroom floor
Is lit. See the gold sheen on the over-
Whelmed grasses? See the starched ruff of the hedgerow?
And the dancers are dressing. They tease
Their toes into shoes. Tease their breath into stays:
Stay the moment. Stay the luck. Stay, stay, the fields
Are full of rain and baby's breath. These will
Fashion the heart, and the heart fastened to the sleeve
Will break fire as the redbird did this morning
Bursting his small buttons against the glass. The glass
Was not black-hearted. It was an innocent pretender.
It took to itself the idea of sky and the bird bought
It, played his brave swan dive into our palms.
So let us wear it. Let us wear the bird like
A boutonniere to remind us that caution snares
Nothing. O the cautious are caught in the net
Of their cares: *Stop, No Turn, Leave Your Shoes*
At the Door. Please Don't Spit on the Statue and
Tokens Go Here. But the bird rode his cheer up.
Rode the high wire of his cheer up. Left
Without counting the cost his spittle-bright snail
Trail for the rain to erase, for the wind to wash
Out. Booted his small body beyond the Beyond.
Now the wrecked grace of the morning trails
Its tattered clouds. But they are flowers.
The pink flowers of Maryland turn softly above us.

Courting the Famous Figures
at the Grotto of Improbable Thought

A jester or a buffoon might play with demons and not pay.
A jester might see these vines as bell ropes
And drag a sound from them. A commiserating sound. Rain
Or bird fall through wet air. The fall of angels.

God watched the angels fall. It was something like
A thunderstorm: out of keeping with the season: spectacular
In the way it dressed the sky: a surge of romantic music
Overplayed: and then that feeling of famous entry.

A jester might deliver a benediction but who would believe him?
Would God? Would God in his sad figure here? Would you?
The statue is very cold. It is lodged in the cave
Like a pocket mirror reflecting our distress. The boy

Lies dead on his mother's legs: his arm dropped:
Like the head of a flower dropped: the stalk snapped:
The head trailing: the mother's face afflicted
With the indecency of it all: the undressed moment:

The exposure of the broken motion. The statue might have been
A lamp if the stage had been managed properly. But
The double figure is only a shrunken reproduction: one
Of a thousand rabbit-like offspring of a more solemn notion.

The original that the madman leapt over the velvet ropes
To disfigure with his busy hammer keeps lurking
Behind it and laughing. Or is that the madman laughing?
There are no ropes here. The boy is lost to the wet shades.

He sleeps a child's sleep: his face bearded by the milk
He drank before bed: the milk beard: the beard before the man
Beard that these walls have grown. They have grown a face.
Not like the face of Moses who broke the tablets of the law.

Not like splendid Moses who came down from the mountain
And burned the golden calf to powder. And made the sons
Of Israel drink it. A magnificent rebuke. A meal
Of such extravagance it had to be concocted from phantoms.

But more like the face of a bearded lady: vaguely indecent:
Sexual in its longing. Water braids down the swollen vines.
And the moss is thick and singular: frosted with pale
Fluorescence. The story seems to be about overblown failure.

A passion for the morose. For perpetual rains. A heavy
Foot on the pedal prolonging the melancholic denouement.
The candles quaver in the long shadows the pines lay down.
And the saints assume their assigned postures: Posture

Of swallowing the ribald joke whole. Posture of turning
The quiet cheek for yet another slung tomato or stone.
One saint pulls his plaster cassock up with a coy motion,
His perfect lips pouted, exposing for us the leg wound

That was healed: a figure of the sweet lyric. Tra la la la.
Because it worked out wisely. Because it worked out well.
At his naked feet the sparrows scatter seed on the wet
Pavement. The child who sells holy trinkets feeds them....

Now, see. We came for a revelation. A thick-headed
Generation: needing a miracle. We came for a show of Mercy.
Something as tangible as the trees' dropped cones: full
Of like kind: of like seed. Something we could juggle

Or plant against the coming need. We came with our orders
In hand. We came with our costumes. We had practiced
Our roles for a long time: the songs of suffering heroically
Endured, the parables and puns, conundrums and complaints,

The pantomimed fables and two-headed jokes, limericks and jigs,
The whole bag of tricks designed to catch God off guard
And relieve him of one or two of his multitudinous gifts.
We followed the rules. Though your ankles are weak

We climbed the steep cliff to the main attraction. The Goliath
The grotto is named for: The Lady of Improbable Thought.
The Lady of Prolonged Silence. The Lady of Strange Shape
That the hand of Anonymous hammered from the stone.

High-wrought hand. Awkward but unique. Possessing the power
Of Origins. How many years did it contend with the Lady?
How many hammer blows to uncover the brow? The neck?
The giant cloaked breasts that paraded above us?

The Lady is a ship stalled and willing for the wait.
The gulls cut from her skirts cross over. She is a ship
And figurehead in one: a blind form: having no pupils.
(Unless we are her pupils? The sight she has forsaken?)

We followed the rules. *We followed them all.* We moved
About her skirts: the blank tablets of her nomenclature:
We skirted the main issue. We did our tricks
And waited for applause. Was that it in the bird flurry?

Was that it in the yellow rag trussed to the tree?
Water dripped down the stone. There was the smell of dirt
And the smell of small illegal fires. There was
Expectancy and need: the clearing they made in the trees

Through which something might have moved. But
There was a deficit in the faculty of the Imagination.
We were no lions of Judah. We had no slingshot.
Not one smooth stone with which to reach her monstrous

Forehead. Wherever we stood the Lady looked away:
As if she were listening to something that made no sound:
Her sideward habit shouldered by the art we've lost:
The assumption of the scene behind the scene: that pulls

The action forward: that gives it meaning. Couple
Vengeance with those things we cannot subtract. Coins
In the saints' cups. Smiles like weak flowers. Solace
Sliding as we did back down to this plaster strong-

Hold of saints.... *O Lady. O Lady. Around us an ocean.*
A field of disinterest. But still we push forward.
We bow, we bend. We keep moving. *Though we feel nothing.*
We keep moving. Here in the theater of public longing.

The Music Lesson

Collect of white dusk. And
The first epistolary drops
Strike sparks from the leaves,

Send up the sweet fragrance
Of the Far Gone. Where
The maple fell in another rain

Red and white umbrellas
Hold back the weather: sun
And moon and the seasonal

Displays the four hands
Keep time to: the telling
And the told. Back and forth:

Back and forth: the lesson's
Passion is patience. Through
The domino tumble and clutter

Of the pupil's untutored touch
The metronome keeps
A stiff upper lip, pays out

Its narrow train of thought,
While above, God,
Gold carrion in a lit frame,

Rehearses His reproach, one-
Noted. Final. The unnegotiable
Real estate of absolute loss:

Discipleship's cost. O hands,
Hands, doing their work:
The steeple hat of the dunce

Is stiff with recalcitrant
Notes, but still the ghost hammers
Leap. And luck makes an entrance

In this: See: lightning
Partitions the dusk—illuminating
Our brief lease—and with

A cocksure infusion of heat
Luck lays hands on
The boy's hands and prefigures

The pleasure that will one day
Possess this picture for good.
This is the stone the builders

Rejected. Pleasure. *Pleasure.*
The liquid tool, the golden
Fossil that will come to fuel

In lavish and unspeakable ways
All the dry passages
The boy does not now comprehend

Or care for. And then his
Stricken hands will blossom
Fat with brag. And play.

Of Ancient Origins and War

And briefly stay, the junketing sparrows, briefly,
Briefly, their flurries like small wine spills,

While the one divides into two: the heart and its shadow,
The world and its threat, the crow back of the sparrow.

Near the surface, beneath the soft penetrable mask—
The paste of white blossoms slurring the broken ground—
Alarm begins its troubled shoot: *the fruit tree*

Beareth its fruit: a load of old fruit tricked out
By the scattershot light, figured gold by the furious light.

The will given early to the dream of pleasure falters,
In a slurry of scent, in a posture of doubled-over gold,
And then there is the rift, the sound of cloth tearing

As the crow shoots up—fast with apparent purpose—
Splitting wide the leaves of a tree we cannot name,
Growing by a gate made from another tree, a gate

That cries as it swings, the cry of the broken safety.
The world and its haste, the world and its threat,
The here where we will die coming closer. All the sorrow

Of it, sparrow trouble, sparrow blow, our hands
These sparrows, quick and quick, but tippling now,

Toppling, bellies full of the bad seed the hair spilled
When it broke from the last comb it was locked into.
The will given early to the dream of pleasure falters.

And now, in the dark, listen, in the dark
The tulip poplar is singing, the leaves are singing,
The clear high green of a boy's imperilled soprano.

The moon is rising, the sound like wine spilling.
The boy will grow a beard, the boy will be bearded.
The bird will dive back down in perfect execution.

The damaged will can only watch and wonder
Through a surface alarmed with dust.... And so now.
And so that now. We are in the trouble of a sleep

We did not dream of. And the shadows of the trees
Are breaking. The shadows of the world's broken vessels.

Garden of Flesh, Garden of Stone

The little white throat has his head in the boy's ear.
        Maybe he has found some seed in it. Or maybe
he is telling the boy a secret, some sweet nothing.
        Or maybe he has mistaken the rimmed flesh,
taut and sweet as the skin of a fig, for his bathing dish,
        and is about to dive through the pale sky
reflected in it, lengths of blue, lengths of gray,
        yards and yards of quarried white. And the boy,
who is made of stone, who has stood still for a long time,
        pissing in the stone basin, seems this morning
in the peculiar light to be leaning his large head,
        barely balanced on a narrow neck, toward the sparrow,
as if he likes the soft sewing motion of the beak
        within his ear, the delicate morse of the white throat,
a bird as plain as dust, but swift-witted and winged,
        and the possessor of the saddest of all calls,
five slow notes that bring to mind a whole garden
        of fruit trees in winter, trunk after scarred trunk,
the mist stiff in the branches, and the sound
        of single drops of water striking the charred ground
as desolate as the sound of the boy's fountain
        dripping and dripping into the drained basin
long after the water has been shut off. Today the basin
        is full. The boy stands above it, one hand on his hip,
as if he were a gunslinger, the other in front,
        guiding the narrow stream of water up and out
in a spinning arc that changes color in the light
        and tosses when it hits the flat surface of the water
a handful of silver seed up. This seems to be
        the source of the boy's smile, this and some
teasing riddle the bird has dropped in the boy's ear
        that the boy turns over and over. Now the bird
hops to the boy's shoulder. When he whistles,
        as he will in a moment, his chest will puff out,
and the patch of feathers at his throat will echo

the pouched whiteness of the boy's belly,
a purse of stone crossed by roses, tall roses, long overgrown,
        the dark blooms lapping and lapping at the boy's flesh,
and then, one by one, diving slowly sideways,
        distracted by their own swooning reflections
in the water. The boy is roughly fashioned,
        the chisel marks still visible, but this belly
the flowers fall for is impossibly beautiful.
        The sun has bleached it, and the wind has buffed it,
until it is a perfect rind of fruit, or the perfect curve
        of the moon on nights when it is full and hangs
over the neglected trees behind the boy,
        the pocked stone matching the pallor of the boy's skin,
white gone dusky, shallow water in a shallow basin,
        and the pale hands, too, that move over and under
as they wash themselves in it, the water sighing
        as it falls.... Five notes. Five slow notes.
This is the song of the white throat. Five notes
        so high and sad, and so like a boy's whistle,
they press on a spot deep in the throat, deep
        where the cords band the bone and the breath,
and the boy made of stone shivers. The boy looks up.
        Why has he never heard this song before?
He likes the strangeness of it. He likes the ghostly trees
        that rise up around him like the remnant
of a garden he once stood in but has forgotten—
        a garden in which there was no fountain.
He likes the charred smell of wet dirt and the mist
        that slides across the blackened branches
in strands as slow and milky as the horned snails
        that come out at dusk and drag their silver trails
down the walk. He likes his shaking body
        and the taste of old fruit on his tongue....
But abruptly the song stops. The trees step back.
        Now the bird is all business. The bird snaps
his beak as he moves brusquely up and down
        the boy's long arm, measuring it as if it were
a length of cloth, smoothed and ready for cutting.
        The bird snaps. And the boy, who is made of stone,

who is crudely fashioned but still lovely,
      slowly, slowly shifts his weight from his back foot
to his front, which unbalances his narrow shoulders,
      and makes the stream of water, arced like a bow,
arrowless, but ready, thin to a thread,
      and the water in the basin go slack. The boy
wants the bird to stop. He wants the bird
      to come back and croon in his ear, like the lover
he has never had, or he wants the white throat
      to go for good. He will not stand for this cutting.
Why should he? Doesn't the bird know of the pact?
      The privilege the boy was granted when the one
with somewhat clumsy hands chose to make him
      not of wood or of gold or of pale washed flesh
but of stone? No cloth would ever darken
      his body with shadow. No shadow would grow
from his feet and loop its noose around him,
      the way it does those other boys, the ones
behind the wall, who with rocks and shrill shouts
      bring down bird after singing bird. He traded
that pleasure for this. To stand harmless
      and never move. To never move and never be dressed,
as even this white throat is, in his own shroud.
      Why did he listen to the bird's song? What is this
weight of stone in his belly? Where is the one
      with heavy hands? How will he call him?
And what, when he raises his small voice
      for the first time, will that voice sound like?

II

Field Song

What stands? The walnut:
  the tower of story
    dark with crows,

The leafy way station
  for doomsayers:
    Say nay, say no,

Say the morning comes in
  with a silver spoon
    and the spoon rattles

In a cup because
  the child is gone.
    But still the child

Stands, the way a statue
  does in the mind:
    or in a field: a fawn

Figure with a filigreed
  grin: there beside
    the walnut and the way

Of passing things:
  the wide road down
    the middle of it all.

The middle ground
  gives way and we
    are on either side,

As in a game:
  You're it. You're not.
    You're out. Arms up

You stand,
  with those taken
    for all they're worth:

The lace of Anne,
  the rods of gold,
    the stalks made from iron:

Their color drains away,
  but still they hold
    on: a dry feast:

The way things fast
  toward their absent
    forms: go in hunger.

Go in grace.

Dead Doe

for Huck

The doe lay dead on her back in a field of asters: no.

The doe lay dead on her back beside the school bus stop: yes.

Where we waited.
Her belly white as a cut pear. Where we waited: no: off

from where we waited: yes

at a distance: making a distance
we kept,
as we kept her dead run in sight, that we might see if she chose
to go skyward;
that we might run, too, turn tail
if she came near
and troubled our fear with presence: with ghostly blossoming: with
    the fountain's
                            unstoppable blossoming
      and the black stain the algae makes when the water
                          stays near.

We can take the gilt-edged strolling of the clouds: yes.
But the risen from the dead: no!

The haloey trouble-shooting of the goldfinches in the bush:
                         yes: but *in season:*

kept within bounds,

not in the pirated rows of corn,
not above winter's pittance of river.

The doe lay dead: she lent
    her deadness to the morning, that the morning might have weight, that
        our waiting might matter: be upheld by significance: by light
            on the rhododendron, by the ribbons the sucked mint
                loosed on the air,

by the treasonous gold-leaved passage of season, and you

from me / child / from me /

from . . . not mother: no:
but the weather that would hold you: yes:

hothouse you to fattest blooms: keep you in mild unceasing rain, and
    the fixed
             stations of heat: like a pedaled note: or the held
                breath sucked in, and stay: yes:
stay

but: no: not done: can't be:

the doe lay dead: she could
do nothing:

the dead can mother nothing . . . nothing
but our sight: they mother that, whether they will or no:

they mother our looking, the gap the tongue prods when the tooth is
    missing, when
             fancy seeks the space.

The doe lay dead: yes: and at a distance, with her legs up and frozen,
    she tricked
             our vision: at a distance she was
             for a moment no deer
at all

but two swans: we saw two swans
        and they were fighting

or they were coupling
　　　or they were stabbing the ground for some prize
　　　　worth nothing, but fought over, so worth *that*, worth
the fought-over glossiness: the morning's fragile-tubed glory.

And this is the soul: like it or not. Yes: the soul comes down: yes: comes
into the deer: yes: who dies: yes: and in her death twins herself into swans:
fools us with mist and accident into believing her newfound finery

and we are not afraid
though we should be

and we are not afraid as we watch her soul fly on: paired
as the soul always is: with itself:
　with others.
　　　　Two swans....

Child. We are done for
in the most remarkable ways.

∽

Arguments of Everlasting

My mother
gathers gladiolas: the little tubes
shout and clamor: a poppling
of unstoppled laughter: the guileless leaps
and quiet plosives
of the fountain when it is working: when
mechanics and meaning are flush
and untroubled. Not like
my brother's stammer: speech and its edicts
broken by that intruder
between tongue and tooth: something
winged: of insect color.
          My mother
gathers gladiolas. The gladness
is fractured. As when
the globe with its thousand mirrors
cracked the light. How
it hoarded sight: all the stolen perspectives
and the show of light
they shot around us: so that
down the dark hall the ghosts danced
with us: down the dark hall
the broken angels.
          What keeps
the grass from slipping? The steep
grass? Like my brother
it imitates the stone's arrest: *this done*
this done and nothing
doing. In the face of the wind
it plants its foot
and fights its own going:
a travelling line
of adamance.
          My mother,
the doves are in full cry

this morning.
The leaves are heavy
with silken grieving: soft packages
of sorrow: cacophonies
of sighing. It is a pretty
thing, a pretty thing,
the light lathered like feathers,
and the day's spendage
beginning. The flag unspools its furl
above the school,
pulsing out and out: a wake
of color on the air:
blue: red: blue:

and how white the sky is. How white.

Wild Turkeys: The Dignity of the Damned

Because they *are* shame, and cannot flee from it,
And cannot hide it, they go slow,
One great variegated male and his harem of four wild hens

Halting our truck as they labor
To cross the road into the low fields they are indentured to.
They go slow, their hearts hardened to this;

Those laughingstock, shriveled, lipstick red hearts—
Swinging on throat and foreneck
Beneath the narrow heads that are the blue

Not of the sky but of convicts' shaved skulls—
Have been long indurated by rains and winds and filth
And the merciless exposures of the sun.

They do not look up, they do not fly—
Except at night when dark descends like shame,
When shame is lost to dark, and then,

Weak-winged, they heave themselves
Into the low tree roosts they drop from in the morning,
Crashing like swag-bellied bombers

Into the bare fields and stingy stands of trees
They peck their stones and seeds from.
Yesterday they were targets, but now they go slow,

As if this lacuna between winter and spring, still gray,
But full of the furred sumacs' pubescent probings,
And the faint oily scent of wild onion vials crushed open,

Gave hope to even them, or as if they knew
All seasons to be one, the going back,
The crossing over, the standing still, all the same,

When the state you defend is a lost state,
When lurching into an ungainly run
Only reminds you that there is nowhere to run to.

And this movement, this jerking
Of these heavy goffered carapaces forward,
This dumb parading that looks at first glance furtive,

Like skulking, the hunkered shoulders, the lowered heads,
Reveals, as we watch, the dignity that lines
Of pilgrim-sick possess as they halt toward some dark grotto—

A faith beyond the last desire to possess faith,
The soldier's resolve to march humpbacked straight into death
Until it breaks like oil over him

And over all that is lost.

Divining the Field

Through the body of the crow the finch flies:
Small yellow-green patch of flower springing
Up in the weedy field: of briefest flight.
The flower will be shot dead by the coming cold
Or by the woman's disregard. Her forgetfulness
Arrows him the way Saint Sebastian was arrowed:
Poor man stuck with a hundred bony wings, laddered,
The stripped shafts trembling, as if Sebastian
Had been instructed to climb his own flesh
Up into the high regard his skewered sight
Was planting there: Crow's Nest: House of the Spy.
Regards grow up like trees. The thing Sebastian
Was thinking when he died: a leafy assemblage
With a driven core: swift monument of oak or stone
The heart passes through, the way the finch
Passes through the body of the crow: the lord
Of highness. From his post the crow shouts
The other hawkers down: sells tickets to
Sebastian's fledging: devours in one gesture
The finch like a piece of fruit: like a roasted morsel.
It is too much to bear sometimes: a tree
Of flame-flung arrows, a bird selling portions,
Our endless lust for spectacle to rouse
The stupored sight. As if the body of Sebastian's
Death were not always with us: This high
White garment of grasses the birds fly through,
Opening with their sharp gold wings
The purple and crimson wounds of the flowers.

Pipistrelles

i.

In the damp dusk
The bats playing spies and counterspies by the river's
Bankrupt water station

Look like the flung hands of deaf boys, restlessly
Signing the dark. Deaf boys
Who all night and into the half-lit hours

When the trees step from their shadows
And the shadows go to grass
Whistle those high-pitched tunes that, though unheard, hurt

Our thoughts. Pipistrelles, little pipes, little
Night pipes, the peculiar
Lost fluting of the outcast heart. Poor heart.

The river's slate waters slide
Silt and grief, the whole destroyed mountain of winter
Over the weir. Never stopping,

Sometimes slowing, but never stopping. And
Along the banks the skinflint trees
Clasp their weak heat. Well, they are a touchy choir,

A confused congregation, breathing
The thin air of our unteneted world. The sun pales,
The leafy dogma goes, and we are left

To our freedom. But do we see now
The world as it actually is? Or merely another world?
A world within a world? Perhaps

In spring, when the dogwood
Slowly discloses its hoard of pale mothlike blossoms
It is the mind that mulls

The sap—perhaps it is the mind
That makes its worlds
And the miracles therein.

ii.

The bats resemble the deaf.
But they are not deaf. They live by echoes, as we do.
Negotiate by echoes. Send signals out

And field the reflections on the wing. And only
Great fear will hang them
On the piano wires we string to test them,

Dead certain of our right to know
At any cost the mechanism of another's flight.
Even blindfolded, even painted

All over with nail polish, the bats will manage
Those wires pulled free
From their instrument, from their sound, will play

Around them a makeshift music
So lovely the pianist's fingers will falter in envy,
And only great fear will hang them.

But it is different with us. Fear in us
Is central. Of the bone. It is our inheritance.
Our error. What flies back at us

From rocks and trees, from the emptiness
We cannot resist casting into,
Is colored by the distortions of our hearts,

And what we hear almost always blinds us.
We stumble against phantoms, throw
Ourselves from imaginary cliffs, and at dusk, like children, we

Run the long shadows down. Because the heart, friend,
Is a shadow, a domed dark
Hung with remembered doings. A night feeder—moths,

Fur over the tongue and the wet jewel of blood,
The cracked shells of insects
Split on the wing. And elsewhere, by connection,

Blood draining from the perfect cut
That brings the rabbit down, a slow singing out,
As in a dream, the blood sliding,

As the water of the overflowing creek does, sideways
In its brief bid for freedom,
While above, something wings away.

iii.

We are not birds. Despite our walls covered
With winged men, we are not birds.
And all that is birdlike in the bats

Is also deception. They have
No feathers, no beak, no high-pitched heart.
Their wings are skin. Skin! Stretched

From shoulder to foot like the cloth
We nailed to wood to build
Our doomed medieval contraptions for flight,

Or like our taut sheets, the high-strung skin,
The great single wing of sex we lean on
But we are not birds. All that is birdlike

In us, in the bats, is illusion.
There is nothing at all of the bird in us....
Except for flight. Except for flight.

Cry of the Jay

An admiral
riposte: the blue dress of the jay
on the high fence: his high way
of regarding down the otherness:
the blank looks
that would defeat.
The sky is not so blue
or so contained:
bird breast a cobalt pistol: shot:
the small heart exploding
into raucous cry: the whole
packed-in warmth of June focused
and set free.
Free borne this fiery
fracas of bird and flesh and
smoldering air:
free freight
the light that slides like struck sand
down: though still the light
stands above: as light will do:
behaving in lustrous banks
of unseamed richness.
Unlimited
gratitude might take such
a shape: *We are within. It is the only*
place: Sanctuary of sameness
made strange by hard-hit
sight: gathering place
of the wayward protocols
dressing now for dinner
after their dressed-down
state.....

The jay is above

it all. As the seed
of the self will be:
If that other
larger call
comes in.

⌒

The White Pilgrim: Old Christian Cemetery

The cicadas were loud and what looked like a child's
Bracelet was coiled at the base of the Pilgrim.
It was a snake. Red and black. The cemetery
Is haunted. Perhaps by the Pilgrim. Perhaps
By another. We were looking for names
For the baby. My daughter liked Achsa and Luke
And John Jacob. She was dragging her rope
Through the grass. It was hot. The insect
Racket was loud and there was that snake.
It made me nervous. I almost picked it up
Because it was so pretty. Just like a bracelet.
And I thought, Oh, the child will be a girl,
But it was not. This was around the time
Of the dream. Dreams come from somewhere.
There is this argument about nowhere,
But it is not true. I dreamed that some boys
Knocked down all the stones in the cemetery
And then it happened. It was six months later
In early December. Dead cold. Just before
Dawn. We live a long way off so I slept
Right through it. But I read about it the next
Day in the Johnsonburg paper. There is
This argument about the dead, but that is not
Right either. The dead keep working. If
You listen you can hear them. It was hot
When we walked in the cemetery. And my daughter
Told me the story of the White Pilgrim.
She likes the story. Yes, it is a good one.
A man left his home in Ohio and came East,
Dreaming he could be the dreamed-of Rider
In St. John's Revelation. He was called
The White Pilgrim because he dressed all
In white like a rodeo cowboy and rode a white
Horse. He preached that the end was coming soon.
And it was. He died a month later of the fever.

The ground here is unhealthy. And the insects
Grind on and on. Now the Pilgrim is a legend.
I know your works, God said, and that is what
I am afraid of. It was very hot that summer.
Even the birds were quiet. *God's eyes are like*
A flame of fire, St. John said, *and the armies*
Of heaven.... But these I cannot imagine.
Many dreams come true. But mostly it isn't
The good ones. That night in December
The boys were bored. They were pained to the teeth
With boredom. You can hardly blame them.
They had been out all night breaking trashcans
And mailboxes with their baseball bats. They
Hang from their pickups by the knees and
Pound the boxes as they drive by. The ground
Here is unhealthy, but that is not it.
Their satisfaction just ends too quickly.
They need something better to break. They
Need something holy. But there is not much left,
So that night they went to the cemetery.
It was cold, but they were drunk and perhaps
They did not feel it. The cemetery is close
To town, but no one heard them. The boys are part
Of a larger destruction, but this is beyond
What they can imagine. War in heaven
And the damage is ours. The birds come to feed
On what is left. You can see them always
Around Old Christian. As if the bodies of the dead
Were lying out exposed. But of course they are
Not. St. John the Evangelist dreamed of birds
And of the White Rider. That is the one
The Ohio preacher wanted to be. He dressed
All in white and rode a white horse.
His own life in the Midwest was not enough,
And who can blame him? My daughter thinks
That all cemeteries have a White Pilgrim.
She said that her teacher told her this. I said
This makes no sense but she would not listen.
There was a pack of dogs loose in my dream

Or it could have been dark angels. They were
Taking the names off the stones. St. John said
An angel will be the one who invites the birds
To God's Last Supper, when he eats the flesh
Of all the kings and princes. Perhaps God
Is a bird. Sometimes I think this. The thought
Is as good as another. The boys shouldered
Over the big stones first, save for the Pilgrim.
And then worked their way down to the child-
Sized markers. These they punted like footballs.
The cemetery is close to town but no one
Heard them. They left the Pilgrim for last
Because he is a legend, although only local.
My daughter thinks that all cemeteries
Have a White Pilgrim, ghost and stone, and that
The stone is always placed dead in the center
Of the cemetery ground. In Old Christian
This is true. The Ohio Pilgrim was a rich man
And when he died the faithful sunk his wealth into
The marble obelisk called by his name. We saw
The snake curled around it. Pretty as a bracelet.
But the child was not a girl. The boys left
The Pilgrim till last, and then took it down
Too. The Preacher had a dream but it was not
Of a larger order so it led to little. Just
A stone broken like a tooth, and a ghost story
For children. God says the damage will be
Restored. Among other things. At least
They repaired Old Christian. The historical
Society took up a collection and the town's
Big men came out to hoist the stones. The boys
Got probation, but they won't keep it.... I
Don't go to the cemetery anymore. But once
I drove past and my babysitter's family
Was out working. Her father and mother were
Cutting back the rose of Sharon and my red-haired
Sitter, who is plain and good-hearted, was
Pushing a lawn mower. Her beautiful younger
Sister sat on the grass beside the Pilgrim

Pretending to clip some weeds.   She never works.
She has asthma and everybody loves her.
I imagined that the stones must have fine seams
Where they had been broken.   But otherwise
Everything looked the same.   Maybe better....
The summer we walked in the cemetery it was hot.
We were looking for names for the baby
And my daughter told me the story of the White
Pilgrim.   This was before the stones fell
And before the worked-for restoration.
I know your works, says God, and talks of
The armies of heaven.   They are not very friendly.
Some dreams hold and I am afraid that this
May be one of them.   The White Rider may come
With his secret name inscribed on his thigh,
King of Kings, Lord of Lords, and the child
Is large now . . . but who will be left standing?

Percival

Percival comes. If I pretend he is not here
He grows larger in the barn, filling all the shadows,
And then I cannot go in to feed the cows

And I hear those who give milk crying for milk
And I see their hearts, like children's palms,
Opening and closing in the garden. Even in winter

I keep the garden. And Percival, who never looks
At flowers, taps his fingers on the water
That has frozen in buckets in the barn.

I hear that tapping. Even as I heard him coming,
Last night through my sleep, through the snow,
His heavy black coat dropping like wings.

III

Past the Stations

A washed corpse, the body of rain-drenched trees
That below my window darkens further. In
Remembrance. Grave blanket of dusk over it.
Cold sheet of mist over it. Death a bird shadow
On the sill. This is the plot of my consideration.
The copse below my window, the small wood
Without an oracle, with no significant episode.
It is a hand's breadth. It is a small ache.
The hand knocks at the window. The window opens.
The smell of wetted dirt and wild fruit steps
Up. Blood fruit: Blood apples. Bitter to the taste
And good. The hand reaches out and the sheet
Slips down. Sigh of silence and a cat passing,
Pale as a ghost, pale as peeled fruit, pale as
Its own pale claws looking for another find....
Like caskets, trees can be counted, together
Or apart. If you stand above the woods, the tree
Is one. It is many, if you walk below. Many,
If you step past the stations of your thought
And number your steps. Smaller and smaller.
The faculty of expansion decreasing. The faculty
Of breath decreasing. The rain withdrawing
With a whistling hush.... Somebody thinks
Or somebody turns. Into what? Into what?

Silver Lake

Fast-locked the land for weeks. Of ice we dream.
Of ice and the low fires the fishermen feed on Silver Lake.
All the lakes are called silver here, though none are that.
And this one now is white and shot through with fishing holes.
It looks like the blasted back of one of those huge turtles
That summer drags out of the weeds with the lure of sweeter bogs.
They lumber with the ponderous slowness of some interminable sermon
And they are easy game for the long-legged boys in pickups
Who hack their backs with axes to make thick soup. Years
In that soup. Unseen years and depth to mull the blond meat
That my great great Uncle Lusty in England made his fortune from.
But that is another story. Now the lake—with its toppled shrine
And the memory of its lone heron, seasonal and proud—is sealed;
And on these frigid fog-bound days the sun comes late,
If at all, comes like a slow yellow age stain on linen,
Or like the muted blare of the fluorescent lights you can see
Through the smeared windows of the Gulf Station garage.
Sometimes it has the iridescence of spilled oil, and always
In the fog you can look straight at it, as you can look
At the sun in Medjugorje, and it will not burn your eyes,
Though here we are not changed much by such sights.
Once you were alone on the ice. Too cold for the rest.
All day the wind was rank with the metallic smell of old snow,
Blowing over and over itself, tangling like lost laundry,
And even the hungry packs of snowmobiles—that sound
As they cross the cornfields with their shrill chain-saw whine
As if they are felling whole forests—were silent.
Dusk was coming on. And I watched you for a long time.
I was in the open, though you did not see me, did not turn
To where I stood in the high grasses the weather had stained black.
You sat on your three-legged stool by a numb fire, your boot
Cocked on the coughed-up collar of ice the awl leaves,
And waited for the fish to spring your trap, spring
The pink plastic flag that made me think of the lawn flamingos
In the yard of the Kinkel's Corner antique shop. Few stop there

Because the highway's hairpin curves are deadly and blind,
But one morning I stood among the flocks of those plastic birds
And the statues posturing in the yard. Virgins and trolls.
Saints and satyrs and naked women with no arms. "Things
That keep and do not change," as the proprietor told me.
And he pointed to the painted figure of a shirtless slave
Up the narrow walk to his house. "See that colored boy," he said.
"I've had him sixty years, and all he needs is a little varnish."
The lower rims of the man's eyes belled forward and were very red
And it was impossible not to look at that soreness....
You sat for so long on the ice my tongue went numb in my mouth
And I woke to see you paying your line out slow as a delicious thought
Into the circled dark. There was a pause before whatever contract
You made with the darkness was complete, the wind repeated
Its wolf whistle in the reeds, and then the prisoner was released—
The orange-winged, green-and-black striped perch flew up, flew fast,
Iced by the fire's light, scattering bright hot pellets as it flew,
The way the priest scatters holy water during the Asperges
At Easter Vigil. And when you put your hand on the fish
I felt how it burned your flesh, burned for the two worlds to meet....
I don't lie to myself. This is what men love the best.
The thoughts they deal from the dark. Better than any woman's flesh.

Distraction of Fish and Flowers in the Kill

People fish the kills here. Black, the kills, with shade,
Moist with shade, and the graveyard odors, the graveyard hush,

The hush of weedy distracted flowers, grass flowers, bush flowers,
Flowers of savor, and those of ill repute.

And beyond, there is always the Island beckoning, to destroy or save,
The lure of the Island, though there is nothing on it

But fireweed and gravel, and between here and there the water
Is deep, the water is deep between.

Fireweed grows where things have burned. The day
Squats with its magnifying glass. The boy in blue shorts squats

On the stones burning ants with his glass, and fireweed, which is not
The color of fire, grows in profusion. Fireweed is purple,

As in shrouds, as in *to destroy or put an end to.*
This we understand. This thing on our hands we would be free of,

One crime or another, the plotted errors, all the dumb-show passages
We play over and over. The unrhymed passages

That call up the chief complaints: Chiefly the wind's fault. Chiefly
That of the Boy Actor....

The water's lights go off and on and the Island beckons.
There seem to be many hands waving. There seem to be many voices saying,

Jump now, before the fire gets you, the heart fire, the brain fire.
We are holding the sheets, holding the bedclothes.

And, yes, the air is full of white stuff: feathers or grave wrappings:
Something broadcast wholesale to the wind. But the warm water

Shackles our ankles, and the wrong ideas are firm
In the body: the idea that harm can hasten

The coming of good. That rain can make a lasting forgetfulness. The non-
Swimmer's reckonings that weaken the ankle. Poor

Lily-white ankle, dreaming it will step forward
As if for the first time.

The Witnesses

The Witnesses come again. They come to my mind
Before they come to the door. The young man wears a red scarf.
And the old woman is soft in the head. We sit on the porch
And she fans the waves painted on the *Watchtower*'s cover.

The waves are blue as rebellion. "The ocean," she says,
"See here . . . the ocean . . . the ocean is full of dirt . . .
And it is going...." And she is gone. Stares blindly
At the spot where two drab deer made the baby laugh

By eating dead bushes. He thought they were cows. "Moo,"
He said. "Moooo." He names things by their sounds.
The young Witness picks up the dropped conversation.
He plies a soft black book. Is pledged to persuasion.

Once he was a Papist, but now is not. He frowns
At the statue of Mary covered with bird lime. "The signs
Will come," he says. "The signs, and then the End.
Only the chosen will stand." My mind lies quiet.

I hear the crows barking. The ocean is going.
And the trees in good faith are drinking our poison.
How dark the night is and high up. Starless
With ignorance. There through the low branches

The turning river shines gold as a prize ribbon,
Gold and proud as a seal of approval. But the water
Has no fish in it. And the watchtower has no beacon.
Or the beacon is broken. The beacon limps over the ocean

Like the mind of an old person coming to thought
And receding.... Or like the flight of a damaged bird....
My sister had a bird once and my cousin got it. He
Pulled its feathers out. He stood under the street lamp

And pulled its feathers out. Then he pitched it
Into the air again and again, whistling as it plummeted
Like a falling star.... *O kill the bird! Kill it!*
Be done with it!... O do . . . not kill . . . the bird....

"Don't let the Witnesses in," says my husband. "They
Pollute the place. Talk to them on the porch," he says.
"Or better, at the bottom of the hill." Posted with signs
The fence row there guards the game preserve the hunters

Flush deer from. They shoot the deer dead on the road
And then strap the bodies upside down to the tailgates
Of their trucks, so that the deer's necks arch back as ours do
In sex, but soft, soft.... *The Witnesses come again.*

Guest Place

Hospice of wanting. Hindmost of the day. Back
Of the cedar bush. The guest place in the shadow

Where I lay down my longing, little cat, little bird.
Of split leaves the scratched dirt smells, of mice,

And of the blue shade that salvages the forehead, milk
Shadow, sweet liquid brimming the flesh's shallow basin.

But there is the other shadow. The hostile shadow
Outside that spills blackly over the face: shadow

Of the wind's rebuke dashing a paper down the street:
Flint shadow striking the bushes so that laughter

Sprays out: atomized: a shrill gaudiness: our words
Coming back to us as cheap thrill: cheap perfume....

The nursling cries for milk. For milkiness.
The crow cries for his own poor behavior.

The fledged effort stumbles on the air. The air
Is thin and powdered with the leaves' exhalations:

A series of soft blows: the soft finery pumped
Out like dispensations. But hard to catch: hard

To catch the breath.... Under the bush of dogged
Mildness we lie. And think of the busyness all around.

The unthinking cruelty. Our own genius for harm.

The Pear Tree

The jewel called citrine is yellow. And so are my pears.
And so is the eye of the crow. No, that is not right.
Now I remember. The crow's eye is black, like his feathers.
Not red or yellow or gold. And the pears this year

Are green and misshapen. But you can see this for yourself,
Pears like the organs of chickens, plucked for cooking.
The rains did them in. The rains came in early, bringing
The cold, and the crows came soon after, squalling and fretting,

A hundred crows, a thousand, day after day, too many
To count. They set up house in the elms by the bog
And now the yard smells of dogs. They bring the dusk
In early. The little pears can't hold it off. Their lamps

Are low on oil. They shed no light on the dirt I dig....
I wanted the ring for my wedding. The *citrine*. But the man
Said it was too expensive. It was an old ring,
Lying on black cloth, locked under glass. I wish you

Could have seen it. The color of my pears in good years
When they steep, fat and sweet, in their own hot grease,
Or of the sun when it comes in behind the falling rain,
A blurred gold, an amber spill that turns the dark rain

Into a coat of many colors, a hundred colors, a thousand,
As many as the colors in the songs of God. Or in
The finch's feathers.... *Bird like a jewel....* Do you know
The kind I mean? Yellow and green. The bird I bury is one—

The man's pet. *The plaything of the man's heart.* The pretty one
In the silver cage with the silver bell and the rope
Plaited from strips of silk. I held him this morning
Folded on his back like a piece of fine linen. I stroked

And I sang. His wings dusky as the leaves of the pear tree,
The rings of his feet bright as the pears when the pears
Are gold.... Now his song will be forgotten.... *Poor little pears*
The rain has bullied.... Poor little finch I killed

And bury.... Poor little heart with its ruined gardens....
Do you want to see them? Five are the gardens. Daily
I count them. Here are the sunflowers, bagged of their boast.
The rains did them in, stole their seeds and their size. And this

Is where the tulips stood, red tulips, yellow tulips, white.
Their heads were all topped by the deer and the rabbits.
I put out poison from my little pail to stop the moles
But it did nothing. One garden, two, and garden three—

Drowning now in rust—is the small patch of strawberries
That the man first bedded in the middle of the grass
Where the little plants looked like something spilled,
So I dug them up, but they have not taken to their place

By the gate—the only berries were snagged by the crows.
And the fourth garden is the garden of the graves of pets:
One-armed monkey, a voiceless cat, a rat called Goliath,
Toads, snails . . . and now in the shoebox that darkens in the rain,

The finch of many colors, a hundred colors, a thousand,
Too many to count. This garden thrives in any weather,
Here beneath the pear tree, the last of my gardens,
Fast by the bog. But now the pears I count on are green

And misshapen. They have no breasts or feathers, nothing
Soft to stick your fingers in. Even the crows don't want them....
Filthy birds. *Look at them.* Black as the waters of the bog
They brood over. Liars' tongues are black like that.

And so are the songs of Darkness. And so is the skirt
I smothered the bird with. Shrouding the cage,
Bringing the dusk in early.... How loud the rain is.
How loud the sound. Listen to it falling. It falls

On the shovel. It sounds like stones hitting tin cans
Lined up on a wall. Ping, ping, ping. Or like bullets.
And the sound gets louder.... *It was the rain....* No . . . no...
It was . . . *the cries* . . . the vocables morning and evening....

I could not hear myself think.... My thoughts were all broken.
The bird's cries were so sharp . . . sharp as the saw grass....
Or the pronged sumacs that spring up everywhere and threaten
The gardens.... I have to yank them out by the roots

Or they eat up all the ground.... *What else is there to do?*
Count the gardens, count the graves, count the fallen jewels.
But it all . . . seems . . . *uncountable* . . . the varying hues.
This little bird alone had a thousand colors. And now

Its mate will die. That is what the man told me.
As one finch goes, so goes the other. As one garden,
The others follow. One crow, then a thousand.
A thousand days to the heart's desire. A thousand

Hands to its ruin. And the sounds I make, they, too,
Are a thousand. I flap my arms and call in the dark
To the bird I hated. While the rain falls faster
And the moon comes up like a pail of poison. And the voice

Of the bog grows louder and louder. Do you hear
The singing?... *O foolish woman. O foolish woman,*
What were you thinking? Which of your thoughts
Was so important? Put down your spade. Leave off

Your weeping. The rain will keep falling. The crows
Will keep flying. Sit on the ground and wait. Sit
On the ground and wait. Perhaps the bird you planted
Beneath the pear tree . . . will become . . . another pear tree.

Petition

These are the long weeks. The weeks
Of waiting. Let them be
Longer. Let the days smolder
Like the peat slung
In plastic sacks by the greenhouse
And let the seedlings not rush
Into growth but climb the air slowly
As if it were a ladder,
One small foot at a time.
Let the fetid smell of bone meal
Be the body unlocking
As the river does, slowing to a hazy laze
That pulls the boaters in
And makes the fish rise up. And
As the wide-wheeled yellow tractors
Roll along the highway,
Stalling traffic in their wakes,
And the dust from the playing fields
Settles over us like pollen,
Like the balls dropping softly
Into our mitts, let
The willow's love of water—
Its dark and beaded rain—
Be the only storm we long for.

Botticelli's St. Sebastian

I have seen a robin cock his head so,
Listening for the change in weather,
Feeling in the field's pale grass turning paler
The moment of his own departure.
I have seen the bird throw his whole body
In the air, and go, the small bird go,
And the bared ground at once lose heart,
As if taken by a sudden grippe.

And I have seen blond wood, fine-grained
As this stripped flesh, seen the long
Boards of strong wood—when bound fast
And bitten by the drill—spew up phrases
As curled and extravagant as Sebastian's gaze,
The way the lover does at consummation,
Lost to himself and to the world, but still
Safely shaded by the tree he rose from.

I have seen, I have seen the lake's heart
When the rain comes through, when the water's
Dark flesh is driven, *I have seen* the heart
Move like a doe through the woods, move
Like a stunned doe, deeper and deeper,
Through trees that turn and close behind her,
The way water closes over a dropped stone,
Or a torn limb, or a lasting wound....

O, the forgotten traveller!

All Wild Animals Were Once Called Deer

Some truck was gunning the night before up Pippin Hill's steep grade
And the doe was thrown wide. This happened five years ago now,
Or six. She must have come out of the woods by Simpson's red
    trailer—

The one that looks like a faded train car—and the driver
Did not see her. His brakes no good. Or perhaps she hit the truck.
That happens, too. A figure swims up from nowhere, a flying figure

That seems to be made of nothing more than moonlight, or vapor,
Until it slams its face, solid as stone, against the glass.
And maybe when this happens the driver gets out. Maybe not.

Strange about the kills we get without intending them.
Because we are pointed in the direction of something.
Because we are distracted at just the right moment, or the wrong.

We were waiting for the school bus. It was early, but not yet light.
We watched the darkness draining off like the last residue
Of water from a tub. And we didn't speak, because that was our way.

High up a plane droned, drone of the cold, and behind us the flag
In front of the Bank of Hope's branch trailer snapped and popped in
    the wind.
It sounded like a boy whipping a wet towel against a thigh

Or like the stiff beating of a swan's wings as it takes off
From the lake, a flat drumming sound, the sound of something
Being pounded until it softens, and then—as the wind lowered

And the flag ran out wide—a second sound, the sound of running fire.
And there was the scraping, too, the sad knife-against-skin scraping
Of the acres of field corn strung out in straggling rows

Around the branch trailer that had been, the winter before, our town's
    claim to fame
When, in the space of two weeks, it was successfully robbed twice.
The same man did it both times, in the same manner.

He had a black hood and a gun, and he was so polite
That the embarrassed teller couldn't hide her smile when he showed
    up again.
They didn't think it could happen twice. But sometimes it does.

Strange about that. Lightning strikes and strikes again.
My piano teacher watched her husband, who had been struck as a boy,
Fall for good, years later, when he was hit again.

He was walking across a cut cornfield toward her, stepping over
The dead stalks, holding the bag of nails he'd picked up at the
    hardware store
Out like a bouquet. It was drizzling so he had his umbrella up.

There was no thunder, nothing to be afraid of.
And then a single bolt from nowhere, and for a moment the man
Was doing a little dance in a movie, a jig, three steps or four,

Before he dropped like a cloth, or a felled bird.
This happened twenty years ago now, but my teacher keeps
Telling me the story. She hums while she plays. And we were
    humming

That morning by the bus stop. A song about boys and war.
And the thing about the doe was this. She looked alive.
As anything will in the half light. As even lawn statues will.

I was going to say as even children playing a game of statues will,
But of course they *are* alive. Though sometimes
A person pretending to be a statue seems farther gone in death

Than a statue does. Or to put it another way,
Death seems to be the living thing, the thing
That looks out through the eyes. Strange about that....

We stared at the doe for a long time and I thought about the way
A hunter slits a deer's belly. I've watched this many times.
And the motion is a deft one. It is the same motion the swan uses

When he knifes the children down by his pond on Wasigan road.
They put out a hand. And quick as lit grease, the swan's
Boneless neck snakes around in a sideways circle, driving

The bill hard toward the softest spot.... All those songs
We sing about swans, but they are mean. And up close, often ugly.
That old Wasigan bird is a smelly, moth-eaten thing,

His wings stained yellow as if he chewed tobacco,
His upper bill broken from his foul-tempered strikes.
And he is awkward, too, out of the water. Broken-billed and gaited.

When he grapples down the steep slope, wheezing and spitting,
He looks like some old man recovering from hip surgery,
Slowly slapping down one cursed flat foot, then the next.

But the thing about the swan is this. The swan is made for the water.
You can't judge him out of it. He's made for the chapter
In the rushes. He's like one of those small planes my brother flies.

Ridiculous things. Something a boy dreams up late at night
While he stares at the stars. Something a child draws.
I've watched my brother take off a thousand times, and it's always

The same. The engine spits and dies, spits and catches—
A spurting match—and the machine shakes and shakes as if it were
Stuck together with glue and wound up with a rubber band.

It shimmies the whole way down the strip, past the pond,
Past the wind bagging the goosenecked wind sock, past the banks
Of bright red and blue planes. And as it climbs slowly

Into the air, wobbling from side to side, cautious as a rock climber,
Putting one hand forward then the next, not even looking
At the high spot above the tree line that is the question,

It seems that nothing will keep it up, not a wish, not a dare,
Not the proffered flowers of our held breath. It seems
As if the plane is a prey the hunter has lined up in his sights,

His finger pressing against the cold metal, the taste of blood
On his tongue . . . but then, just before the sky
Goes black, at the dizzying height of our dismay,

The climber's frail hand reaches up and grasps the highest rock,
Hauling with a last shudder, the body over,
The gun lowers, and perfectly poised now, high above

The dark pines, the plane is home free. It owns it all, *all*.
My brother looks down and counts his possessions,
Strip and grass, the child's cemetery the black tombstones

Of the cedars make on the grassy hill, the wind-scrubbed
Face of the pond, the swan's white stone....
In thirty years, roughly, we will all be dead.... That is one thing...

And you can't judge the swan out of the water.... That is another.
The swan is mean and ugly, stupid as stone,
But when it finally makes its way down the slope, over rocks

And weeds, through the razory grasses of the muddy shallows,
The water fanning out in loose circles around it
And then stilling, when it finally reaches the deepest spot

And raises in slow motion its perfectly articulated wings,
Wings of smoke, wings of air, then everything changes.
Out of the shallows the lovers emerge, sword and flame,

And over the pond's lone island the willow spills its canopy,
A shifting feast of gold and green, a spell of lethal beauty.
O bird of moonlight. O bird of wish. O sound rising

Like an echo from the water. Grief sound. Sound of the horn.
The same ghostly sound the deer makes when it runs
Through the woods at night, white lightning through the trees,

Through the coldest moments, when it feels as if the earth
Will never again grow warm, lover running toward lover,
The branches tearing back, the mouth and eyes wide,

The heart flying into the arms of the one that will kill her.

IV

Three Cows and the Moon

We were playing baseball on the hill by the cow field.
It was late March. The trees were getting dark.
The moon was coming up. We couldn't see it yet.

It came up almost like a sound behind the stand
Of scrub trees to the South. And it would be full.
I knew this because I hadn't slept for two nights.

The bull and the two heifers had their heads stuck
Between the fence slats so they could watch us. We were
Throwing a tennis ball and hitting it with a stick.

My son was wearing one of those flimsy plastic jackets.
It had a broken zipper and it was yellow,
The color the moon would be later. The color

Also of my daughter's hair, which was uncombed.
Uncombed or not she is always beautiful.
It's the funny laugh and those long legs.

But she can't catch. She is awkward. She kept
Dropping the ball and she couldn't do anything
With the stick that my son swung like a soldier.

It was an old branch with the bark peeled off.
I picked it up from the poplar that was felled
During the hurricane. For two years the tree bloomed

Where it lay, flat out on the ground. It didn't
Know it was dead. It was like a garden
Someone planted and then abandoned. A pitiful thing,

The trunk split clean in two and the fallen branches
Still blooming.... It gets cold fast in March
And dark. The three of us were playing ball. And dusk

Was coming out of the ground. I heard a poet say this.
That darkness doesn't come down but rises up.
And he was right. It gets the ankles first. It circles

The ankles like flood water gradually filling
The basement of a house. Dark water full
Of unnameable things. It circles the thin trunks

Of the trees, a black current, soft as the current
Of fear that almost always runs through me,
Or the scent of a bruised flower eddying outward....

Our old cocker was playing, too, yapping in his god-awful
Way, running back and forth and stealing the ball.
We don't shave him so his mane was flying.

We'd chase him and tackle him to get the ball back,
Smearing our faces with dirt and grass,
And we didn't notice when the cows started playing

Their own game. It might have been when the moon
First came up behind the trees: it was huge
And close, a blurred ruddy color. The color of a body

Just stepping from a bath. Or a body pulled
From icy water. When I was a child we used to swim
In the Little Pigeon River at just this time

Of year when the ice was still floating in it.
We could stay in the water for only a minute.
We'd hold our breath and jump and when

We were hauled out seconds later our skin was red,
Our skin was hot, even in the cold air.
The moon was like that. Or like a child's cheek

Struck by a parent—no, because it didn't hurt—
And the cows were playing their game. They'd come
Together with their flat noses touching, and then

Very slowly they'd start turning like a wheel.
The cow field is pitched steeply to the East
And to the West. The runoff from both directions

Leaves a black stain down the middle of the field
And even in hot times a trickle of water.
The cows drink from it, though it's probably not clean

Because the septic bleeds into it. The turning
Was difficult because of the field's steep pitch
But the wheel kept moving. It moved faster and faster

In ragged circles. Always clockwise. Three
Thick-legged bodies, matted with dung and grass,
Held together as if by invisible ropes. Up and down

The field, snorting and thumping, the laboring
Wheel would move. As if to cover all the ground,
As if to break up the hard ground for planting,

And then all at once the wheel would shatter,
The way a wooden wheel shatters when it strikes rock,
Spokes flying off in all directions. The cows

Would stagger to their corners, shaking their heads.
And then after awhile they'd make another circle.
Sometimes our hearts are stone. Sometimes not.

When the moon came up ruddy, the sky around it
Was blue, though the field was very dark.
And the top of the sky was dark. The sky

On the opposite hill to the North was white,
It was white, but also very dark. It gets
Dark faster on the hill because of the trees.

The trees get bigger at night and shut out the light.
The darkness seems to leak out of them. It leaks
Out of the ground and out of the trees, and it

Is as beautiful and sharp-edged as the leaves
Of the mandrake flooding the swale at the hill's base.
The dark was cold. Our shoulders were warm.

But the dark was cold. And it was getting harder to see.
But still the cows kept turning. There was the low
Cry of winter birds left back like dumb children

Kept behind in school. And the bats were whistling
Around us, whistling and shuttling, as the moon
Came up over the trees, smaller and clearer now.

It looked like a pale bird moving through the air
That smelled of old batteries, a ghost bird
Beating its wings above the ghost light of the bull's horns

Rising and falling through the field's dark rooms.
My son would swing the peeled stick back and forth,
Back and forth, as if he were swinging a scythe,

The rhythmic flash of the yellow wood writing and erasing
Faint messages on the dark in answer to those
Sent out by the slow dance of the bull's horns.

Once there was a sacrifice for sin. And it
Was a bull like this one. A first born.
Once there was a garden of god. And we were in it.

I raised the bull and he had a man's face.
His mother died right after he was born in the field
Back of the house in the town of Harmony

Where we used to live. She dropped him by the creek,
And then walked off and lay down to die.
Maybe she didn't want him to see her. She made

A terrible sound. Like a ship that was going down.
A foghorn sound. It was late morning and I was sleeping.
I didn't want to get up. I didn't know what

The sound was. It kept breaking into my dream,
Which was about a window that had been shattered
By rocks. The window was black and large, and as it

Opened wider and wider it became the mouth of a lion,
Out of which something issued, something small,
Maybe some bees, or maybe the song of a child.

By the time I went to find the sound it was too late.
The heifer died of milk fever. The other
Cows stood off staring. They have stupid eyes.

And I took the bull so he wouldn't be made into veal.
I bought the bull who had never seen his mother
And tied him to a stick and fed him with buckets

Of a watery white solution. And he grew bigger.
And his face was human. You can take my word for it.
There are four angels standing at the four corners of the earth.

The sky turns light all over just before it blacks out,
And the moon gets clearer and clearer as it
Gets smaller. The dark comes up and then it comes down

All at once in a black rain. We were losing
Our faces. There was no color now to the sky
And the cows kept moving. The bull had a human face.

And there was a hum starting up. Not the moon,
Though that might have been making a sound.
Not the bats nor the softening ground

The cows were working. But there was something.
Maybe the high whine of the cold working in.
Or maybe there were wings. We were watching now

And not playing. Watching the heavy circles
We could barely see move over the wet field
And we were listening. Maybe there were wings.

Maybe the cows had wings under their legs.
Or arms. Maybe they had arms with hands
Under their wings. Maybe the dark was winged.

The bull had no mother and so I raised him.
He had a human face. And the wheels moved
Over the field. The spirit was in the wheels

And we were watching though we were going blind.
We were watching as if the wheels were a cart
And we'd ride it through to its destination.

And then we started moving again. Throwing the ball
That we could no longer see. The yellow
Of the ball, the yellow of the horns, the yellow

Of the dog tearing back and forth between us
All blacked out now. Our skin was alive
And we were getting hot while the sky got colder

And the moon turned to salt, turned bright and fine
As salt or oil, a river of oil sliding by.
There was one poplar in the field and sometimes

We'd grope for it, as if for safety. We'd
Put our arms around the rough bark and press our faces
Close. The poplar held itself perfectly still

Like a seer, the top leaves visible against the sky.
But then the game would pull us back. We fell
Toward the sounds of each other. The shapes

Of each other. Whatever we were without bodies.
We were playing blind and the moon was rising.
The spirit was in the wheels. And there were eyes

All around. No movement in the poplar. The sound
Of flesh being punched. Of fur being torn.
The air all dizzy and kicked-up. A holy insect

Buzz in the air. The high whining buzz of the cold
Catching fire. The smell of frozen manure
And dead flies. Of old grass and new grass. The sound

Of something small crying. There were wheels
All around. And the spirit was in the wheels.
And the children's skin pricked by cold

Smelled of bleeding. And blood tastes of cooked
Flowers. And the ball dropped as if into water.
And the last sound was the sound of the cows stopping

In the final circle. And it was quiet then.
And we were looking up. Light flooding a room.
The four corners of the night all staked out.

The moon high up and small. High up and small.
Perfect like a flower. Or an oracle. Something
Completely understood. But unspeakable.

⌐

Acknowledgments

Grateful acknowledgment is made to the journals and anthologies in which the following poems first appeared.

The American Voice: "The Music Lesson" and "Of Ancient Origins and War";

The Antioch Review: "Cry of the Jay," "Divining the Field," "Field Song," "The Pear Tree" and "Of Royal Issue";

The Cream City Review: "Guest Place";

The Georgia Review: "Arguments of Everlasting";

The Gettysburg Review: "The White Pilgrim: Old Christian Cemetery";

The Kenyon Review: "Dead Doe";

The Journal: "The Column of Mercury Recording the Temperature of Night" and "Distraction of Fish and Flowers in the Kill";

The Massachusetts Review: "All Wild Animals Were Once Called Deer";

New England Review: "Silver Lake" and "Three Cows and the Moon";

The North American Review: "Past the Stations";

The Northwest Review: "Courting the Famous Figures at the Grotto of Improbable Thought";

River Styx: "Petition" and "Wild Turkeys: The Dignity of the Damned";

The Southern Review: "Song";

The Sycamore Review: "Botticelli's St. Sebastian";

West Branch: "Percival";

The Yale Review: "Pipistrelles."

"The White Pilgrim: Old Christian Cemetery" appeared in *The Best American Poetry 1993*, edited by Louise Glück and David Lehman, published by Charles Scribner's Sons in 1993.

"Courting the Famous Figures at the Grotto of Improbable Thought" appeared in *The Best American Poetry 1994,* edited by A.R. Ammons and David Lehman, published by Charles Scribner's Sons in 1994.

"Song" appeared in *The Pushcart Prize XIX.*

"Silver Lake" and "Wild Turkeys: The Dignity of the Damned" appeared in *New Poets of the 90's,* edited by Jack Myers and Roger Weingarten, published by David R. Godine.

I am grateful to The National Endowment for the Arts, The New Jersey State Council on theArts, The Illinois State Council on the Arts, and to The Center for Advanced Study and the Research Board at the University of Illinois for grants that enabled me to complete this book. I also wish to thank The Ragdale Foundation for a residency, and my friend Maxine Scates for her patient and invaluable editorial assistance.

About the Author

Born in Palo Alto, California, in 1951, Brigit Pegeen Kelly teaches in the creative writing program at the University of Illinois at Urbana-Champaign and in the Warren Wilson College M.F.A. program for writers. She has won many awards for her work, including the "Discovery" / *The Nation* prize, the Cecil Hemley Award from the Poetry Society of America, the Theodore Roethke Prize from *Poetry Northwest,* and the 1987 Yale Series of Younger Poets Prize for her first collection, *To the Place of Trumpets,* selected by James Merrill. She has received fellowships from the National Endowment for the Arts, the New Jersey Council on the Arts, and the Illinois State Council on the Arts. Her poems have appeared in many of the country's distinguished journals and anthologies, as well as in *Best American Poetry* and *The Pushcart Prize.*

BOA EDITIONS, LTD.
AMERICAN POETS CONTINUUM SERIES